THE CRUSADES

Peter Chrisp

Wayland

Themes in History

The American Frontier
The Crusades
The French Revolution and Napoleon
Life in the Middle Ages
The Rise of Islam
The Roman Empire

Cover illustration: Detail from a French manuscript depicting the crusades.

Opposite: Godfrey of Bouillon, one of the leaders of the First Crusade, directs an attack on a Muslim cit

First published in 1992 by
Wayland (Publishers) Limited
61 Western Road, Hove
East Sussex BN3 1JD, England

Editor: Mike Hirst
Designer: Joyce Chester
Consultant: Dr Mark Ormrod, lecturer in history at the University of York.

British Library Cataloguing in Publication Data
Chrisp, Peter
The crusades. – (Themes in history)
I. Title II. Series
909.07

ISBN 0 7502 0475 3

Typeset by Dorchester Typesetting Group Ltd
Printed and bound in Italy by
L.E.G.O. S.p.A., Vicenza

Contents

What Was a Crusade?

A twelfth century plan of the Holy City, Jerusalem. To Christians, this was the centre of the world.

'Go forward in safety, knights. With undaunted souls drive off the enemies of the cross of Christ . . . How glorious are the victors who return from the fight! How blessed the martyrs who die in battle!'

These strong words were written in 1135, by a French abbot, Bernard of Clairvaux. He was speaking to the knights of France, encouraging them to set out on a crusade. What was this Holy War that Bernard supported so passionately? And who were the 'enemies of the cross of Christ' that he and the rest of the Church wanted to destroy?

The crusades were fought by western Europeans during the Middle Ages. The First Crusade was launched in 1095 by the Pope, and crusading continued for over two hundred years. All of the crusades set out to fight against the 'enemies' of the Catholic Church. Some crusades were fought against heretics – Christians whose beliefs differed from those of the official Church. Other crusades went out to convert pagans – people in northern Europe who still followed old, pre-Christian religions. But the largest and most important crusades were those fought in the Middle East against Muslims, who followed the Islamic religion.

Between 1095 and 1300, there were at least seven major crusades to the Middle East, as well as many minor expeditions. The aim of these crusades was for Christians to capture and control Palestine, or the Holy Land as the Christians called it. They believed that the very soil of Palestine had been made holy because Jesus Christ had walked upon it. Jerusalem, the city where Christ had been crucified, was especially holy.

Until the seventh century AD, Palestine had been ruled by Christians. It was part of the Byzantine Empire, the empire controlled by the Greeks of Constantinople. Then, between 636 and 650, much of the Middle East was conquered by Muslims, who followed the new religion of Islam.

Islam, which means 'giving in to the will of God', was

A crusader at prayer. He wears a loose coat over his chain mail to keep cool under the hot sun of the Middle East. The crosses show that he is a soldier of Christ.

founded in Arabia by the Prophet Muhammad. He was both a military and religious leader, and, even after his death in 632, his religious ideas continued to spread. By 720, Muslims ruled lands stretching from Spain to India.

Although they conquered many Christian lands, the Muslims did not try to stamp out Christianity. Muhammad told his followers that both Christians and Jews should be

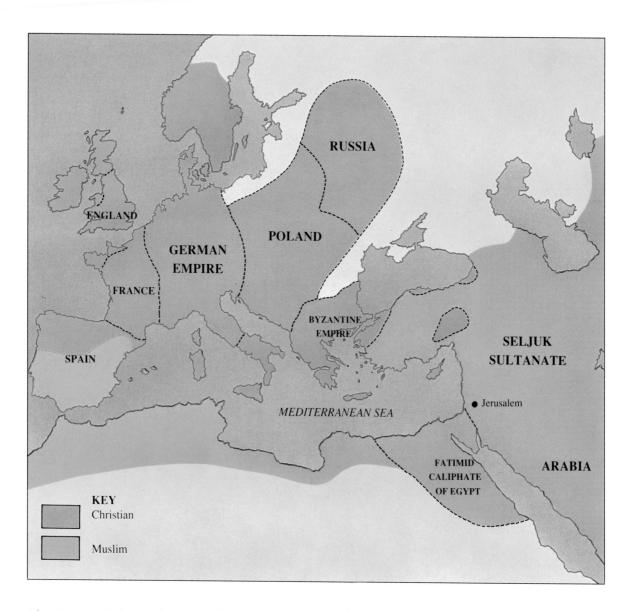

RUSSIA

POLAND

ENGLAND

GERMAN
EMPIRE

FRANCE

BYZANTINE
EMPIRE

SPAIN

SELJUK
SULTANATE

● Jerusalem

MEDITERRANEAN SEA

FATIMID
CALIPHATE
OF EGYPT

ARABIA

KEY
Christian

Muslim

Christian and Muslim lands in the 1090s, on the eve of the First Crusade.

allowed to practise their religions. Like Muslims, they were 'people of the book'. They had a holy book which had been given to them by God. Muslims believed that their holy book, the Koran, was better than the Jewish and the Christian books. But they still honoured the Jewish prophets and Jesus Christ as forerunners of Muhammad. The three religions also shared similar practices, such as prayer and fasting – going without food to please God.

Because the three religions were closely connected, Jerusalem, in Palestine, was a holy city for Muslims as well as for Jews and Christians. Under Muslim rule, the three religious communities lived and worshipped side by side.

While Christian pilgrims prayed in the church of the Holy Sepulchre, built on the site of Christ's tomb, Muslims went to their own holy shrine, the Dome of the Rock. Meanwhile, Jews prayed at the Wailing Wall, all that remained of the ancient Jewish temple.

For centuries, Muslims and Christians were content to live together in the Middle East. It was not until the eleventh century that the Church and Christian rulers, far away in western Europe, decided that Christians, and not Muslims, should now be the people to govern the Holy Land.

The shrine marking Christ's tomb in the Church of the Holy Sepulchre. Every crusader dreamed of visiting this sacred site.

'God Wills It!' – The Call to Arms

Europe in the Middle Ages was a very different place from that of today. The population was much smaller, and there were few towns. Most people lived in the countryside as poor peasants. They farmed the land, although they did not actually own it. Their lives were controlled by a small number of wealthy men – the nobility.

In the eleventh century, poor people were expected to work on the land and leave fighting to the nobility.

In theory, all land was owned by the king of the country. He divided it among his greatest lords and nobles in exchange for their help and support in times of war. The nobles themselves parcelled out some of their land to lesser knights, who also did military service in return. Historians call this system of owning and farming land 'feudalism.'

Medieval knights lived for fighting. This carving of a Norman knight comes from a cathedral in Sicily.

From an early age, the sons of noble families were taught to fight. They learnt to ride a charger (a horse that goes into battle) and use a sword and lance while wearing a heavy coat of armour. Fighting was all they were trained for, and any other work was thought dishonourable. Many knights could not read or write.

Another feature of life in the Middle Ages was the importance of religion and the Church. Almost everyone in western Europe belonged to the Catholic Church. Priests taught that people would be punished after death for the sins they had committed. If someone's sins were great, they would burn in hell-fire for ever. To avoid eternal punishment, people were expected to confess their sins to the Church and then perform penances, to show that they were sorry. Penances might involve fasting or taking part in processions dressed in special clothes.

A common penance was a pilgrimage, a religious journey to a holy place. In particular, people travelled to churches that contained relics, such as the bones of saints. Two important pilgrimage centres were the tombs of St James, at Compostela in Spain, and St Peter, in Rome. But most important of all for Christians was the tomb of Christ, far away in Jerusalem.

Although all the nobility were Christians, they sometimes had disagreements with the Church. The nobles' way of life was based on warfare, yet their fighting was often condemned by the Church. After a battle, knights were expected to confess their sins and then perform penances. Some knights must have felt that the Church was unfair to ask them to do penances simply for doing what they were trained for – fighting. One of the reasons behind crusading would be that it gave knights the opportunity to wage war without losing the support of the Church.

The First Crusade to the Holy Land was declared by the Pope, Urban II, in 1095. He had received a call for help from the Byzantine emperor, the Greek Christian ruler in Constantinople. The Byzantine Empire was being attacked in the east by a fierce Muslim people, the Seljuk Turks. The Byzantines needed reinforcements, and although they did not recognize the Pope as the head of their own Church, they turned to Rome for support.

The Pope wanted to help the eastern Christians, but he soon developed a plan even more ambitious than just sending troops to Constantinople. He wanted to take over the Holy Land itself from the Muslims.

This Greek illustration shows a Muslim camp outside a Byzantine city. The Muslim threat to the Greek Christians was one of the causes of the Crusades.

Pope Urban II proclaims a crusade to a great gathering at Clermont in November 1095. His preaching inspired thousands of Europeans to set off for the East.

The Pope had two main reasons for wanting a crusade:

● A crusade would use the warring knights for the benefit of the Church. While it was a sin to kill Christians, the Pope believed that God would be pleased by the death of 'infidels', or unbelievers. The knights could be saved from hellfire by doing what they were best at – fighting.

● A crusade would also be a way of increasing the influence of the Pope. Urban II was one of a series of Popes who wanted to increase the Church's authority. He hoped that a crusade might even win the Greek Christians over to the Roman Catholic Church.

On 27 November 1095, Urban held a great meeting in a field outside the town of Clermont in France. Many of the knights of France were assembled there. The Pope appealed to them to stop fighting each other. Instead they should unite to rescue Christ's tomb from the unbelievers.

In return, the Church would give the crusaders an indulgence, or pardon, for their sins. By taking part in the crusade, they would shorten the punishments awaiting them after their deaths. Many of the people at Clermont believed

According to one writer, this is how Pope Urban II addressed the crowd of knights at Clermont:

Jerusalem is the navel of the world, a land fruitful above all others, like another paradise of delights. Our saviour lit up this land by his coming and glorified it by his burial. This royal city, set in the centre of the world, is now held captive by His enemies, enslaved by those who do not know God. Therefore she demands to be set free, and calls upon you ceaselessly to come to her aid. Robert the Monk, *The Expedition to Jerusalem* (c.1106)

Was the Pope appealing just to the French knights' religious feelings? Did he suggest other reasons for making the voyage to the Holy Land?

Muslim metalware from Jerusalem. The crusaders expected to find great wealth in the Holy City.

that they would go straight to heaven if they were killed in battle. In any case, since God was on their side, victory was certain. The enthusiastic crowd cried out: 'God wills it!' This became the battle cry of the First Crusade.

The Pope wanted the knights of France to go to the Holy Land, but long before they could organize an official crusade, the call to arms had been carried far beyond Clermont. Europe was gripped by a kind of 'crusade fever'. Urban said that no one too old or weak to fight should set out for the Holy Land, but popular preachers encouraged everyone, not just the nobility, to join in the crusade.

One preacher, called Peter the Hermit, attracted hordes of followers in northern France and Germany. Peasants abandoned their fields before the harvest. Old men, women and children all joined in a great pilgrimage to Jerusalem, which became known as the People's Crusade. Many people had never travelled further than the nearest town before, and had no idea where they were going. One group followed a goose and a goat that they said had been filled with the Holy Spirit and would guide them to Jerusalem!

In the Rhineland, followers of the People's Crusade attacked prosperous Jewish communities. They said that the Jews' ancestors had killed Christ, and so were the enemies of God. They did not need to wait until they reached the Holy Land to kill non-Christians. The whole history of the crusades was to be marked by similar violence against Jews.

When the People's Crusade reached Constantinople, the Greek emperor was horrified to find a large, undisciplined mob outside the city gates – it may have been as many as 20,000 people. Very quickly he shipped the crusaders across the sea into Asia Minor (now the Asian part of Turkey). There, the pilgrimage came to a bloody end, ambushed by Turkish horsemen. Those people who were not killed ended up in Muslim slave markets. When the knights in the official armies of the First Crusade arrived the following year, they found all that remained of the People's Crusade – a huge pile of bones bleached white by the sun.

Peter the Hermit's ragged army is ambushed by the Turks. In this fifteenth century painting, the Turks, shown as European knights, strip the crusaders of their armour and lead them into slavery.

The Journey to Jerusalem

While the People's Crusade met its bloody end in Asia Minor, the knights of the official First Crusade were making their way towards Constantinople. What made these European nobles set off for the east? Why were they willing to travel vast distances to a hostile land where they could be killed in battle or die of sickness or thirst?

In fact, few of the first crusaders can have known what they were really letting themselves in for. In the eleventh century there were hardly any proper drawings or maps of

Knights from all over Western Europe travelled in the vast armies of the First Crusade.

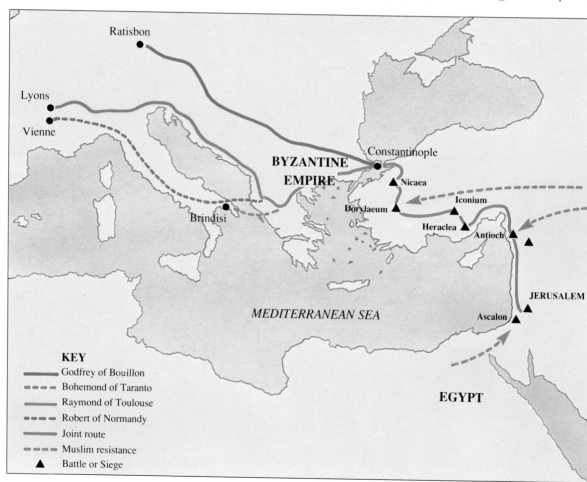

KEY
- Godfrey of Bouillon
- Bohemond of Taranto
- Raymond of Toulouse
- Robert of Normandy
- Joint route
- Muslim resistance
- ▲ Battle or Siege

Hand to hand battles like this one were rare during the crusades. The Muslims, armed with bows and arrows, preferred to keep their distance from the heavily armed knights.

foreign countries, let alone photographs or TV pictures. Few people knew about the climate of the Middle East, or what kind of enemies they would face.

The leaders of the First Crusade had different reasons for going to Jerusalem. Some, like Godfrey of Bouillon and Robert of Normandy, were devout, religious men. Others, like Bohemund of Taranto, were adventurers who hoped to conquer new lands. People thought that it was perfectly reasonable for the crusaders to win wealth for themselves while fighting enemies of the Church. Before a battle, troops were told: 'Unite in the faith of Christ for, God willing, today you will all be made rich.'

The Pope's appeal had been to the knights of France, but the crusaders actually came from many different countries, as far apart as England and Sicily. When the crusaders reached Palestine, Muslims found it difficult to distinguish between the different nationalities, and in many Muslim histories, the crusaders are all called 'Franks', or French.

The crusaders' first problem was raising money. Knights needed horses, armour, servants and expenses for the journey; going on a crusade was a costly business. Many knights on the First Crusade had to borrow money or sell their estates before setting off.

The second difficulty was how to get to the Holy Land. Sea travel was difficult and people were terrified of embarking in small, poorly-navigated boats. So the First Crusade travelled slowly overland.

Above *Crusaders often accused the Muslims of not fighting fairly. Behind these Muslims, who are pretending to be friendly, others are waiting to attack.*

Below *The knights' greatest weapon was a massed charge. Their horses gathered speed until they crashed into the opposing army.*

When the crusade reached the Byzantine Empire, there were quarrels between the westerners and the Greeks. Catholics found the rituals of the Greek Orthodox Church strange, and thought they must be wrong. The Greek Christians in turn were shocked by the rough behaviour of the Franks.

The real problems began when the crusaders had crossed into Asia Minor. Away from the coast, the countryside was barren and mountainous, and the crusaders had to find their own food and shelter. There was also a constant risk of ambushes by the Seljuk Turks, a fierce fighting tribe who had conquered much land.

The crusaders now found that their usual style of fighting did not work so well against Muslims, who fought in a completely different way. European knights would charge at the enemy in a tight group. Head on, such a charge was unbeatable. But the Turks would never meet a head-on charge. They relied on mounted archers, who had lighter armour and faster horses. They would charge up, fire their arrows and then wheel away. The knights' chain mail would usually stop the arrows – at the end of a battle, knights often looked like hedgehogs – but their horses were more vulnerable. It was said that a mounted Frank could bore a hole through the walls of Babylon; but once his horse had been killed, he was helpless.

One favourite Muslim tactic was to pretend to retreat. A small group would flee, acting as bait to lure the crusaders into an ambush. The westerners thought such tactics were treachery. The Muslims, on the other hand, were impressed by the strength of the Franks, but thought that they were incredibly stupid.

When they reached Muslim cities and castles, the crusaders found them much better fortified than any in Europe. The westerners now had to learn new methods of siege warfare. When they came to a Muslim city, they would surround it, and then try to dig under the walls, climb over them with scaling ladders, or knock them down. Enormous machines, such as the mangonel, or catapult, were used to hail rocks, or even the heads of dead enemy soldiers, against the defenders. Both sides used 'Greek Fire', a mixture of chemicals in a pot which burst into flames when it hit anything.

Death in battle was not the only danger facing the crusaders. The scorching climate could be deadly too, and the westerners suffered from heat and thirst. They fell ill

Above *The crusaders had to learn to build wooden siege towers to capture the huge castles and cities of the East.*

Muslim histories of the crusades are very different from Christian accounts. These are two descriptions of the crusaders' capture of Jerusalem in 1099. The first is by a Muslim historian:

The population was put to the sword by the Franks, who pillaged the area for a week. They slaughtered more than 70,000 people. Refugees reached Baghdad during the month of Ramadan. On Friday, they went to the mosque and begged for help, weeping so that their hearers wept with them as they described the sufferings in the holy city, the men killed, the women and children taken prisoner, the homes pillaged.
Ibn al-Athir (1160–1233),
The Collection of Histories

The second description is by a Christian priest who travelled with the crusaders:

Wonderful sights were to be seen. In the Temple of Solomon, men rode in blood up to their knees and bridle reins. Indeed it was a just and splendid judgement of God that this place should be filled with the blood of unbelievers since it had suffered so long from their blasphemies. The city was filled with corpses and blood.
Raymond of Aguilers,
History of the Franks who Captured Jerusalem (c. 1102)

Which words and phrases show the different attitudes of these two writers towards the massacre?

After capturing Jerusalem, the crusaders went on the rampage, killing and looting, stripping the gold from the Muslim holy places.

with dysentery, typhoid and scurvy. At times they were forced to eat weeds, thistles, dogs and rats. So many horses died that some knights had to ride on oxen.

Even though they were weakened by the heat and disease, the crusaders still did penance and fasted regularly, to win God's approval. Not surprisingly, many people reported religious visions!

By 1098, the crusaders had reached the city of Antioch, where they were themselves besieged by a Turkish army. A man named Peter Bartholomew claimed that St Andrew had appeared to him and shown him where the lance that had pierced Christ's side was hidden. A lance was discovered and immediately gave hope to the crusaders, who (after a three-day fast) rode out of the city and defeated the besieging Muslims.

At last, in June 1099, after almost three years of travel, fighting and incredible hardships, the crusaders arrived outside Jerusalem. On 15 July, they forced their way into the city. For two days, they massacred every Muslim and Jew they could find. Then, weeping for joy, they went to Christ's tomb and gave thanks to God. They could hardly believe their victory. Surely, they thought, this must be a sign that God is on their side.

Outremer:
The Land Beyond the Sea

Although they did not know it, the crusaders had invaded the Holy Land at exactly the right time. The capture of Jerusalem seemed like a miracle. But the real reason for the First Crusade's success was that the Muslim rulers were deeply divided.

The Muslim world was bitterly divided. Muslims spent more time fighting each other than uniting against the crusaders.

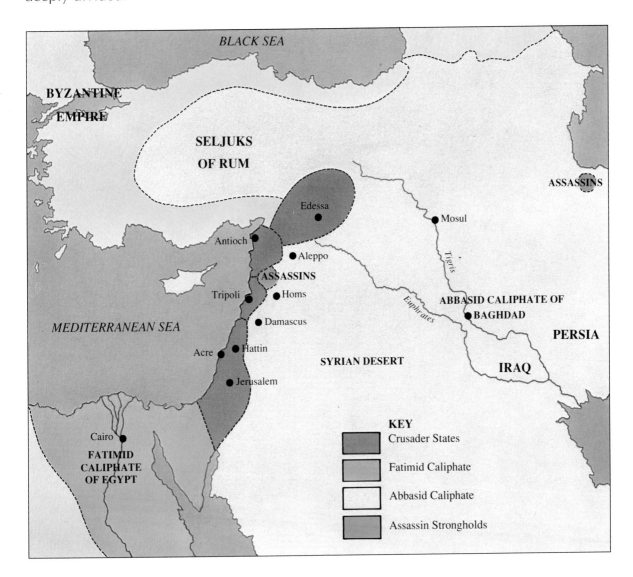

BLACK SEA

BYZANTINE
EMPIRE

SELJUKS
OF RUM

ASSASSINS

Edessa

Mosul

Antioch

Aleppo

Tigris

ASSASSINS

Tripoli

Homs

ABBASID CALIPHATE OF
BAGHDAD

Euphrates

MEDITERRANEAN SEA

Damascus

PERSIA

Acre

Hattin

SYRIAN DESERT

IRAQ

Jerusalem

Cairo

FATIMID
CALIPHATE
OF EGYPT

KEY

Crusader States

Fatimid Caliphate

Abbasid Caliphate

Assassin Strongholds

19

The great dispute in the Islamic world at this time was about who should be caliph – the leader of all Muslims. The majority of Muslims, known as Sunnis, were loyal to the Abbasid family of caliphs that ruled from Baghdad. However, some Muslims believed that only the descendants of Muhammad (through his son-in-law, Ali) should be caliph. These Muslims were called Shiites (pronounced 'shee-ites') because they belonged to the *shia*, or party, of Ali.

One Shiite group, the Fatimids, had seized power in Egypt in 969 and founded a rival caliphate. These Fatimid caliphs waged war on the Abbasids, and, for more than a century, Palestine was the front line between the two groups. At first, it looked as if the Fatimids would win. But in the 1040s, the fierce Seljuk Turks arrived on the scene. They were Sunnis, who supported the Abbasids, and they drove the Fatimids back into Egypt.

If the crusaders had arrived ten years earlier than they did, they would have had to fight the great Seljuk sultan, Malik Shah. But this sultan died in 1092, and his empire broke up as his sons fought one another over who should succeed him. Malik Shah's sons were not very interested in Palestine, as the real centres of Seljuk power were further east, in Iraq and Persia.

A Seljuk mosque in Turkey. As well as being successful warriors, the Seljuks were famous for their elaborately decorated buildings.

While the Seljuk princes fought each other, the Fatimids took advantage of the situation and invaded Palestine again, capturing Jerusalem in 1098. Moreover, to the north of Palestine, in Syria, the local Muslim rulers, or amirs, were also busy quarrelling with each other. They only realized the threat to their power from the First Crusade when it was too late.

It was this disunity in the Islamic world that allowed the crusaders to capture Jerusalem. For as long as the Muslim rulers continued to fight among themselves, the Europeans had a chance of controlling the Holy Land.

In fact, once they had captured Jerusalem, most of the crusading knights returned home to Europe. However, some stayed on to make new lives, and new countries in the East. They formed four new crusader states: Jerusalem, Edessa, Tripoli and Antioch, shown on the map on page 22. Together, these states were called Outremer, a French word meaning 'overseas'.

Outremer was like an armed camp surrounded by enemies. The Turks quickly closed off the route north through Asia Minor to Constantinople, so Outremer could now only be reached from western Europe by sea. Pilgrims and crusaders began to make the difficult voyage by ship, and the settlers in Outremer eagerly awaited the new arrivals who brought news from home.

The new states were governed in a similar way to western Europe. The king of Jerusalem gave estates to his chief lords in exchange for their military services. However, while the feudal system worked well in Europe, in Outremer there were never enough knights for feudalism to work properly.

The Fatimids of Egypt were celebrated for carvings of people and animals, such as this ivory hunting scene.

Outnumbered by the Muslims, the crusader states' survival depended on castles.

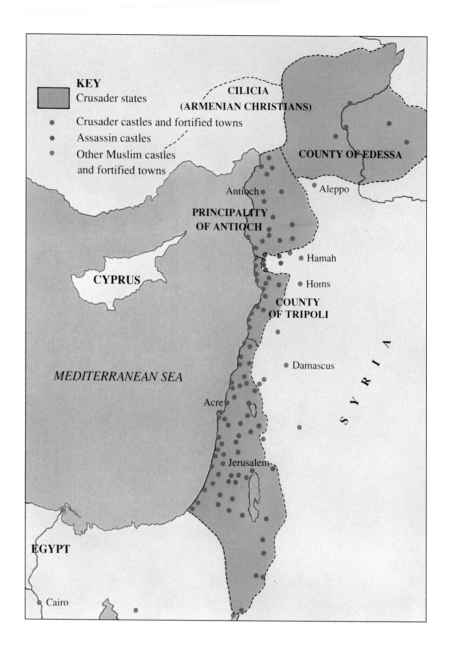

KEY

Crusader states

- Crusader castles and fortified towns
- Assassin castles
- Other Muslim castles and fortified towns

CILICIA (ARMENIAN CHRISTIANS)

COUNTY OF EDESSA

Antioch

Aleppo

PRINCIPALITY OF ANTIOCH

Hamah

CYPRUS

Horns

COUNTY OF TRIPOLI

Damascus

MEDITERRANEAN SEA

S Y R I A

Acre

Jerusalem

EGYPT

Cairo

One solution to the shortage of trained fighters was to set up special military orders. The most famous order was the Knights Templar, formed in 1119 to defend the pilgrim roads to Jerusalem. Its name came from their headquarters, the mosque built in Jerusalem on the site of the Temple of Solomon. The other main order was the Hospitallers of St John, named after its lodging house for pilgrims in Jerusalem. The Germans had their own order, the Teutonic Knights. There was even an order of leper knights, the Order of St Lazarus.

Templars and Hospitallers were fighting monks. They promised never to marry, to live in poverty and always to obey their superiors. Because of these vows, they were more disciplined than ordinary knights and were feared by the Muslims.

The orders also had organizations in Europe, responsible for recruiting new members and for raising money for the defence of the Holy Land. The Templars even acted as bankers for the English and French kings. Because of the shortage of knights, the rulers of Outremer would often give or sell castles to the orders. More and more, they took on the burden of defending the crusader states, and gradually they became rich and powerful. By 1187, they were the biggest landowners in the East.

For the rulers of Outremer, there were drawbacks to the orders. Because they were powerful international organizations, they felt free to do as they pleased and sometimes ignored the wishes of the king. They were also jealous rivals. Sometimes the Templars and the Hospitallers refused to fight side by side.

Above *Templar Knights set off for battle. This is a wall painting from a Templar chapel in France.*

Below *Like western kings, the new rulers of Outremer minted their own coins.*

The survival of the new states depended on castles. In the East, the Franks learned from the Muslims how to build huge castles with round towers and overhanging battlements. They also built fortresses with more than one line of defence. These could be held by a small number of defenders. The crusader castles were important centres of authority. The lord of the castle could control the surrounding district and raise taxes from the local villagers.

The crusaders also strengthened their position by learning to play off the local Muslim rulers around them. They would make truces and alliances, first with one ruler against his rivals, and then with another. As long as the crusaders could

Eastern castles were usually built on hilltops. From these battlements, the crusaders looked out at their new estates.

keep the Muslim world divided, Outremer would be safe.

For most of the local people of Outremer – Syrian Christians and Muslims – life went on much as it had before the crusades. They carried on farming their fields as usual. They simply paid rent, in the form of agricultural produce, to their new European landlords.

From a Muslim point of view, the western settlers were ignorant barbarians. Muslims were disgusted by the Franks' lack of cleanliness and by their habit of shaving their beards. But, as time went by, the settlers were changed by life in Outremer. They soon realized that eastern medicine was far superior to that of Europe, and so they usually employed local doctors. Franks began to dress in silks and cotton, which were much cooler than the wool and leather they had worn before. They also developed a taste for new foods: fruits such as melons, lemons and oranges, spices and sugar – a luxury almost unobtainable in western Europe.

During the many truces, Muslim and Frankish nobles mixed with each other. They found that they had many things in common, in particular a love of horses and hunting. Some Franks learned to speak Arabic. Occasionally friendships were formed with Muslims. But the Franks could never forget that one day they might have to fight their new neighbours.

Muslim silks were highly prized by the crusaders. Many, such as this silk band, found their way back to Europe.

5

Saladin's Rise to Power

In the middle of the twelfth century, a new group of strong Muslim leaders began to emerge and threaten the states of Outremer. The first was a powerful Turkish general called Zengi, who ruled the cities of Mosul and Aleppo. In 1144, he conquered Edessa, the most northerly and vulnerable of the crusader states. Zengi was succeeded by his son, Nur al-Din. Deeply religious, he proposed a holy war, or jihad, against the Franks. Those who took part in the jihad believed, like the crusaders, that God was on their side and that they would be rewarded in heaven if they died in battle.

Against the advice of local crusaders, the army of the Second Crusade laid siege to Damascus, a city which had been friendly to the Christians.

As the Muslims grew stronger, the crusader states began to lose their unity. In particular, there was a split between the Franks who had lived for a long time in Outremer, and those who had recently arrived from Europe. The new arrivals often could not understand the complicated politics of the Middle East, and did not realize how important it was for the crusaders to make alliances with local Muslims.

A portrait of Saladin, the great sultan who united the Muslims and recaptured Jerusalem.

After the loss of Edessa, a Second Crusade was sent to the Holy Land in 1147. But it was a complete failure. In spite of warnings from the local Franks, the new arrivals attacked and laid siege to the Muslim city of Damascus, which had been an ally of Jerusalem. The siege failed and the crusade was abandoned.

The greatest of the Muslim leaders was called Salah al-Din – known to the crusaders as Saladin. He was an officer in the service of Nur al-Din, but he had ambitions to create his own empire. His master sent him to Egypt where, in 1172, he overthrew the Fatimid caliph. When Nur al-Din died in 1174, Saladin made his own bid for power. Through force and diplomacy, his rule spread to Damascus (1174), Aleppo (1183) and Mosul (1186). Outremer was now surrounded by a united Muslim empire.

In 1187, Saladin led his army against the Christian town of Tiberias. To meet the threat, King Guy of Jerusalem summoned the largest army ever assembled in Outremer. On 3 July 1187, at the hottest time of the year, the crusaders marched across a waterless plain towards Tiberias. They were under constant attack from Saladin's archers. Eventually, the troops were so exhausted that they had to rest for the

Like the crusaders, the Muslims believed they were fighting for God. They went into battle with standards carrying inscriptions from their holy book, the Koran.

night, near a place called Hattin. But they had no water and were gasping with thirst. To make things worse, Saladin's men set alight the dry grass around the Christian camp.

By morning, the Christians were in a desperate condition. It was then that Saladin attacked. Although the knights fought bravely, their situation was hopeless. The army of Jerusalem was destroyed and the Fragment of the True Cross, the holiest relic in the kingdom, was captured. Three months later, the victorious Muslims entered the Holy City itself. However, unlike the crusaders who had captured the city in 1099, they did not kill a single one of the inhabitants.

Saladin has often been described as a strong, dashing leader. But what do we really know of his character? These are two descriptions of him, one by a Christian, the other by a Muslim:

This man who campaigned in taverns and devoted his time to gambling, was suddenly raised to sit among the rulers. Overcoming the surrounding countries, he welded many nations into a single monarchy. But the greedy tyrant, not satisfied with these possessions, concentrated all his efforts on an attempt to seize the inheritance of the Lord, Palestine.

Richard of the Holy Trinity,
The Journey of King Richard

The Holy War and the suffering involved in it weighed heavily on Saladin's heart. He spoke of nothing else, thought only about equipment for the fight, was interested only in those who had taken up arms. For love of the Holy War and on Allah's path, he left his family and his sons, his homeland, his house and estates, and chose to live in the shade of his tent, where the winds blew on him from every side.

Beha ad-Din,
Sultanly Anecdotes

Do you think that either of these descriptions gives us a completely true picture of Saladin's character? Why do you think that they are so different?

An English engraving of Saladin, made in 1811. Saladin was the one Muslim leader to be remembered by Europeans.

6

The Third Crusade

Christians throughout Europe were horrified by the loss of Jerusalem. Pope Urban III was said to have died of grief when he heard the news. The new Pope, Gregory VIII, said that the disaster was God's punishment for the sins of the Christians – a common explanation for crusading failures. He called on Christians to repent and start organizing a new crusade.

Three European rulers answered the Pope's appeal: Frederick Barbarossa, the German Holy Roman Emperor, who had been on the Second Crusade and was now almost seventy; Richard I of England, nicknamed Richard the Lionheart; and Philip Augustus of France. Richard and Philip were very different in character. Richard was fierce tempered and outspoken: Philip usually kept his feelings hidden. Richard loved warfare: Philip never took unnecessary risks. The two kings hated each other and spent much of their time quarrelling.

While Richard and Philip were still raising money, Frederick set off overland at the head of a huge German army. But

Crusaders load their ships, before setting out on the dangerous sea crossing to the Holy Land.

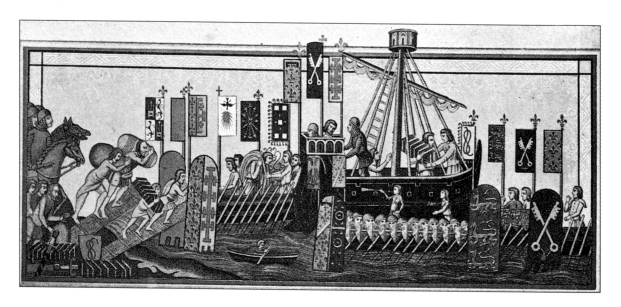

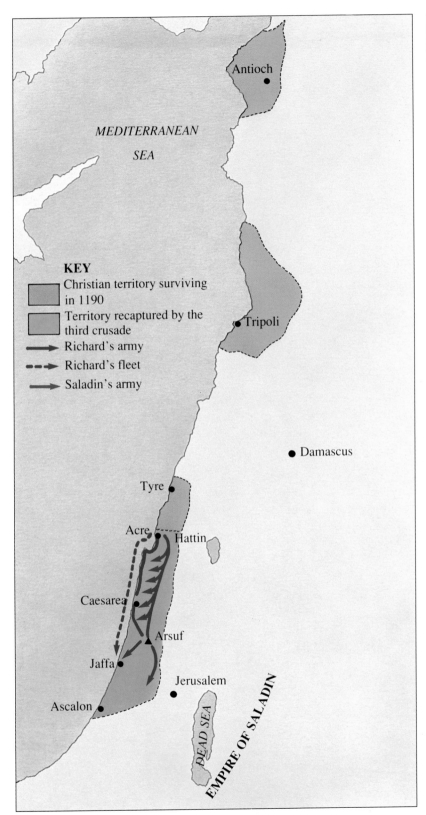

MEDITERRANEAN SEA

Antioch

KEY

Christian territory surviving in 1190

Territory recaptured by the third crusade

→ Richard's army

--→ Richard's fleet

→ Saladin's army

Tripoli

Damascus

Tyre

Acre

Hattin

Caesarea

Arsuf

Jaffa

Jerusalem

Ascalon

DEAD SEA

EMPIRE OF SALADIN

Above *The German Emperor, Frederick Barbarossa, who drowned in a river on his way to fight Saladin. His body was pickled in vinegar and taken to the Holy Land for burial, but most of his soldiers went home.*

Left *King Richard's army marches south, under constant attack from Saladin's forces.*

Although the Church disapproved, all crusading armies included women. During sieges, they sometimes helped in the fighting. This always shocked the Muslims.

the German expedition ended disastrously when Frederick was drowned while crossing a shallow river in Asia Minor. With the Emperor dead, most of his army drifted home.

In July 1190, Richard and Philip set sail for the Holy Land. After a winter spent in Sicily, they arrived the following spring at the crusader camp on the seashore outside the Muslim city of Acre. The crusaders were besieging Acre, although they were themselves under constant attack from the army of Saladin, which was camped further inland.

The Muslims of Acre had already held out for two years, but when the English and French armies arrived, their position became hopeless. The Muslim garrison gave up, starved into submission. They said that Saladin would pay a huge ransom in exchange for their lives.

Philip now returned to France, leaving Richard in command of the Third Crusade. The English king was impatient to march south. When Saladin found it difficult to raise the money for the ransom, Richard had all the prisoners butchered on the plain outside Acre, in sight of Saladin's troops. This massacre brought a new bitterness to the crusade because from that time on Saladin would usually kill all Christian prisoners.

Here are two very different accounts of the massacre of the Acre garrison. The first is by the Christian biographer of King Richard I:

King Richard, always eager to destroy the Turks [Muslims], to defeat the law of Muhammad and defend that of Christ, had 2,700 Turkish hostages led out of the city and beheaded. The king's followers leapt forward eager to fulfil the command, thankful to the divine grace that allowed them to take such a vengeance for the Christians whom these captives had slain with bolts and arrows.

Richard of Holy Trinity, *The Journey of King Richard*

The second description of the fall of Acre was written by a Muslim historian:

The English king broke his word to the Muslim prisoners. He had received the city's surrender in exchange for their lives. He and all the Frankish army fell on them, and as one man, slaughtered them in cold blood. The next morning, the Muslims wanted to see who had fallen, and found their martyred companions lying where they fell. Great grief seized them, and from then on they did not spare enemy prisoners.

Beha ad-Din, *Sultanly Anecdotes*

To the Muslims, the dead prisoners were holy martyrs. What does the Christian writer say was the reason for the killing?

Richard the Lionheart, a great hero to European Christians, but remembered by Muslims as a cold-blooded killer.

After the massacre of the Acre prisoners, Richard's army set off for Jaffa, a city from which he could attack Jerusalem. The crusaders advanced slowly along the coast, where they were kept supplied by Richard's ships. The knights with their vulnerable horses rode nearest to the sea, defended by the infantry, armed with crossbows. All the time the crusaders were harassed by Saladin's mounted archers, who tried to force them to break ranks. But Richard kept strict discipline. According to one account, his troops marched so closely together that you could not throw an apple into their ranks without hitting a man or horse.

Richard stopped off on his way to the Holy Land to conquer Cyprus, whose ruler had imprisoned some English crusaders. Despite the island's strong castles, this campaign took Richard only fifteen days.

After marching for two weeks, at Arsuf, the crusaders finally launched an attack on Saladin's troops. The massed cavalry charge took place at exactly the right moment, and Saladin's army was scattered. After Arsuf, the Muslims were reluctant to meet the crusaders in an open battle.

Richard stayed in the Holy Land until October 1192. He travelled up and down the coast, rebuilding the fortifications which Saladin had destroyed. However, he could not recapture Jerusalem. Twice he came within twenty kilometres of the Holy City, but he realized that it was too risky to attempt a siege.

Even if Richard *had* taken Jerusalem, it was doubtful that the city could have been held. The new crusaders had not come to settle in the Holy Land. Once Richard had gone, what would have stopped Saladin recapturing it?

All the later crusades suffered from this same problem. The kings who led the crusaders could never stay away from their countries for long. Richard stayed sixteen months in Palestine, and while he was away, he almost lost his throne to his ambitious brother John. In the end, Richard made a three-year truce with Saladin and left for home. Under the terms of the truce, the True Cross was returned to the Christians, and pilgrims were once more allowed to enter Jerusalem. Outremer, now only a narrow coastal strip, had been saved – for the time being.

The Decline of Crusading

In the thirteenth century, Christians tried to recapture Jerusalem several more times, but they always failed. Most notorious was the Fourth Crusade, which never even reached Muslim territory. In 1202, the crusaders gathered in Venice, whose rulers had agreed to provide ships for the expedition. However, only a third of the expected forces turned up, and the crusaders found themselves deeply in debt to the Venetians. To pay off the debt, they captured Zara, a city the Venetians had lost to Hungary in 1186. For the first time, a crusading army had attacked a Christian city.

The bronze horses of St Mark's in Venice were looted from Constantinople by the Fourth Crusade.

These mosaics from Ravenna in Italy show episodes from the ill-fated Fourth Crusade. On the left, the Pope gives the crusaders his authority; on the right, they set off, but not to the Holy Land.

Worse was to follow. Instead of sailing to Egypt, their original destination, the crusaders were diverted to Constantinople. They had been offered a vast sum of money by Alexius, son of the recently deposed Greek emperor, if they would help him win power. Although they managed to place Alexius on the throne, he was soon murdered by his subjects. The crusaders then decided to capture Constantinople for themselves. On 13 April 1204, the city fell, and for three days it was pillaged and ransacked. Some of the most priceless treasures and relics of Christendom were stolen. Many of them were taken back to Venice, where they can still be seen today.

The Greek Christians never forgave the Roman Catholics for what had been done. The Byzantine Empire, which had been a defence against Muslim expansion for centuries, never recovered. Between 1300 and 1453, it was gradually conquered by the Ottoman Turks. Today, Constantinople is a Turkish city called Istanbul.

The sack of Constantinople gave crusading a bad reputation. People also began to criticize the use of crusading in Europe. In the thirteenth century, the Pope declared crusades against a Christian sect called the Cathars who lived in southern France. Because the Cathars held different beliefs from the Church, they were persecuted as heretics.

Instead of fighting Muslims, the Fourth Crusade attacked the Greek Christian capital, Constantinople.

Many Catholics believed that the Cathars deserved to be wiped out. But these crusades were criticized for diverting resources from the Holy Land.

Even more controversial were the crusades that were sent against the Pope's political enemies, such as the German emperor, Frederick II. Frederick ruled lands north and south of the Pope's territories in central Italy. The Pope felt threatened by the power of the emperor, and proclaimed a series of crusades against him. These political crusades seemed a long way from the original aims of the Holy War.

Yet some crusaders were still true to the original ideals. King Louis IX of France led two crusades, in 1248-54 and 1267-70. Both were disastrous failures. On the first attempt, the French army, weakened by disease, was surrounded and captured at Damietta in Egypt. Louis was forced to pay a huge ransom for his freedom. The second attempt ended when the king and half his army died of fever at Tunis in north Africa. For once, Christians could not blame the crusades' failure on sinfulness; Louis had led such a holy life that he was made a saint.

The coffin of the saintly French king, Louis IX, is loaded on his ship at Tunis. If someone as holy as Louis could not capture Jerusalem, then who could?

The failure of the official campaigns led to more popular crusades, such as the Shepherd's Crusade of 1251. A man calling himself the Master of Hungary came forward, claiming to have received a letter from the Virgin Mary. The letter said that God was displeased with the pride of the knightly classes. Just as shepherds had first heard the news of Christ's birth, it would be simple and humble shepherds who would be granted the privilege of recovering Jerusalem.

Thousands of shepherds abandoned their flocks and set off from northern France. They never reached the Holy Land – none of the popular crusades ever did. As always, it was the Jewish communities of western Europe that suffered. The shepherds attacked Jews in central and southern France before they were at last forced to disperse.

Meanwhile, the small Christian states of Outremer were still under attack. A new set of rulers, the Mamluks, had come to power in Egypt. One by one, the Christian castles

In the thirteenth century, some Christians began to wonder whether crusading itself was right. Roger Bacon was an English friar and scholar who admired the scientists of Islam. He wrote:

War is not effective against unbelievers since the Church is sometimes defeated in crusades. Nor are unbelievers converted in this way, but killed and sent to hell. Those who survive the wars together with their children are more and more embittered against the Christian faith because of this violence. Besides, the faith did not enter the world by arms but by simple preaching.

Roger Bacon, *Opus Majus* [*The Great Work*] (1268)

Humbert of the Romans was a friar who prepared a report for the Pope on the lack of enthusiasm for crusading:

There are some who say that it is unchristian to shed blood in this way, even that of wicked infidels, for Christ did not act thus. Others say that, although one ought not to spare Saracens, one must be sparing of Christian blood. Is it wise to risk so many of our great men? Others say that it does not appear to be God's will that Christians should proceed against the Saracens. How could the Lord have allowed Saladin to retake the land won with so much Christian blood, the Emperor Frederick to perish in shallow water and King Louis to be captured in Egypt if this kind of proceeding had pleased him?

Humbert of Romans, *Opus Tripartium* [*The Work in Three Part*] (1274)

What reasons do these two writers give for not going on Crusades?

The Mamluk cavalrymen gradually conquered the crusader states. Like their opponents, the Mamluks saw themselves as holy warriors, fighting for God.

and cities fell to the Mamluks – Antioch in 1268, Tripoli in 1289 and, finally, Acre in 1291. As revenge for King Richard's treatment of his prisoners, all the defenders of Acre were killed. The city was razed to the ground. After the loss of Acre, Christians no longer had a port in the Holy Land from which to launch a crusade.

Now that the Holy Land was lost, people also began to criticize the military orders, in particular the Templars. European knights had often resented their power and pride. Moreover, when the Templars returned to Europe after the loss of Outremer, they often behaved like foreigners, making other Europeans suspicious of them.

In October 1307, King Philip IV of France had all the Templars in his kingdom suddenly arrested on charges of witchcraft and heresy. The charges were almost certainly false; the king hoped to get his hands on the Templars' wealth. But they were tortured and forced to confess to the charges. The Templar Grand Master, Jacques de Molay, was later burned at the stake.

In 1314, Jacques de Molay, the Templar Grand Master, and his deputy, Geoffroi de Charney, were burned at the stake for witchcraft. They died protesting their innocence.

8

The Legacy of the Crusades

After the Muslims gained the port of Acre in 1291, the great age of crusading ended. Some Popes still dreamt of recovering the Holy Land, but nothing came of their plans.

The Popes also appealed to western rulers to fight a crusade against the Ottoman Turks, who captured Constantinople in 1453. For the next century the Ottomans seemed unstoppable. By 1529, they had conquered Hungary, and even advanced as far as the gates of the Austrian capital, Vienna. But Europeans still did not renew the Holy War against the Muslims. In the sixteenth century, Catholics and Protestants in Europe were too busy fighting one another. In contrast, the Middle East was strong and united under the Ottomans.

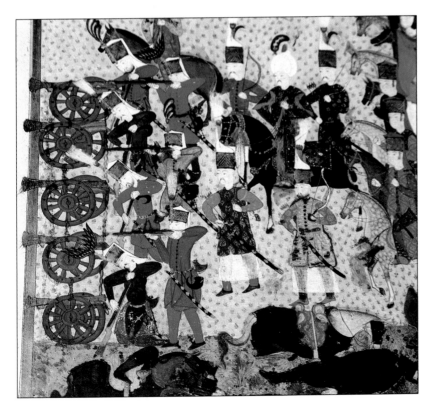

The Ottoman Turks brought the Muslim holy war into Europe. Here they are shown campaigning in Hungary in the early sixteenth century.

From the Christian point of view, the crusades had failed. In the end, the Holy Land was still ruled by Muslims. Yet the most surprising thing is not the ultimate failure of the crusades, but that they had ever achieved any success at all. The knights of the First Crusade would have had no chance against a united Islam. It was only because the Muslims had been fighting each other that the crusaders were able to capture Jerusalem. Once Saladin had united the Muslim forces, Outremer stood little chance of survival.

However, the crusades did bring indirect benefits to the West. In many ways, the Muslim countries were far in advance of medieval Europe, and the crusaders brought many new skills and inventions home from the East.

The most important result of the crusades was the growth of trade. Crusading made the Mediterranean safe for European shipping, and introduced the West to the products of the East – spices and silk for example. More trade led to the

Merchant ships travelling to Outremer. It was worth risking the rough sea crossing for the riches of the East.

development of banks and the growth of towns. Italian cities such as Genoa, Pisa and Venice gained most from the new trade. They had provided the ships that took crusaders and pilgrims to the Holy Land. The Italians understood the new opportunities of the East, and set up merchant colonies in Outremer. They began to build larger, ocean-going ships with more space for cargo.

Before the crusades, ships had hugged the coastlines, navigating by well-known landmarks. From the Muslims, Europeans learnt how to use the magnetic compass and navigate with an astrolabe, which plotted a ship's position by the Sun and the Pole Star. In the eleventh century, most Europeans had been terrified of the sea. At the close of the crusading era, they were setting off across the ocean on epic voyages of exploration.

Contact with Islam also transformed European science and technology. In Palestine, the crusaders learnt how to build giant stone castles, and they brought their new skills back to Europe with them. Muslim doctors, chemists, astronomers and physicists were also much more advanced than their European counterparts, and in the twelfth century, Arabic books, translated into Latin, began to be used in European universities.

A Muslim using an astrolabe, an instrument which could tell the time as well as helping navigation.

Muslim medicine was much more advanced than that of Europe. Here a Muslim pharmacist prepares his drugs.

However, Outremer itself was not a centre of learning. It was in Spain and Sicily that the books were translated and that scientists of different religions met each other. For much of the Middle Ages, these countries were ruled by Muslims, and there were long periods of peaceful contact between a mixed population of Muslims and Christians.

For the Muslims of the Middle East, the crusades had far less importance, and fewer benefits. Muslims in the Holy Land saw the crusaders as barbarian invaders, and had little they could learn from the Franks. Those who lived in Iraq and Persia saw the crusades merely as frontier incidents. They usually left the local rulers in Syria and Palestine to deal with the Christian threat.

The crusades also brought great suffering to many people. Among the victims were the citizens of Jerusalem, massacred in 1099; the European Jews who were attacked by the popular crusades; and the Greek Christians, whose capital was sacked by the Fourth Crusade in 1204.

Despite the terrible bloodshed, in western Europe the religious fervour that inspired many of the crusades has never been forgotten. Crusaders such as Richard the Lionheart and Godfrey of Bouillon were remembered as great heroes whose deeds were celebrated in songs and poems. Even the word 'crusade' itself has taken on a new, general meaning of an all-out effort to destroy something evil. You may still hear people today talking about crusades against poverty, injustice and famine.

Timeline

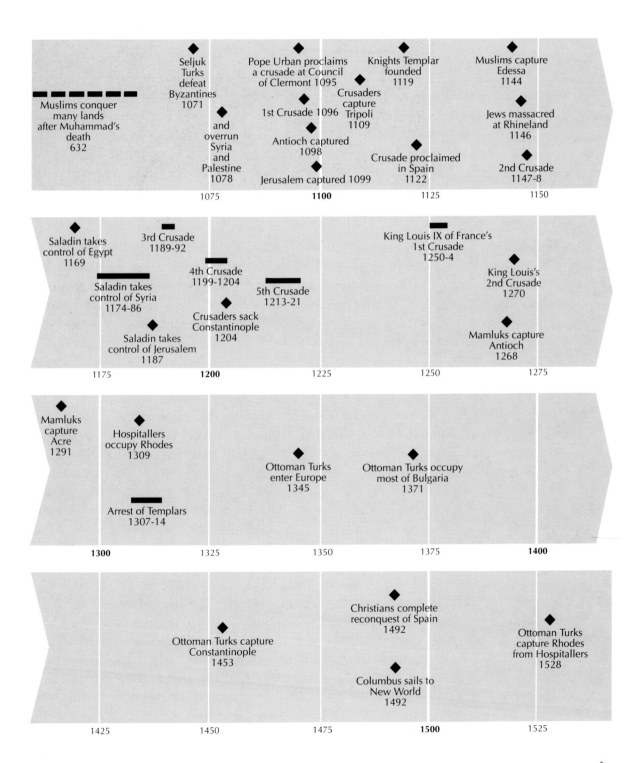

Muslims conquer
many lands
after Muhammad's
death
632

Seljuk
Turks
defeat
Byzantines
1071

and
overrun
Syria
and
Palestine
1078

Pope Urban proclaims
a crusade at Council
of Clermont 1095

1st Crusade 1096

Antioch captured
1098

Jerusalem captured 1099

Knights Templar
founded
1119

Crusaders
capture
Tripoli
1109

Crusade proclaimed
in Spain
1122

Muslims capture
Edessa
1144

Jews massacred
at Rhineland
1146

2nd Crusade
1147-8

1075   1100   1125   1150

Saladin takes
control of Egypt
1169

Saladin takes
control of Syria
1174-86

Saladin takes
control of Jerusalem
1187

3rd Crusade
1189-92

4th Crusade
1199-1204

Crusaders sack
Constantinople
1204

5th Crusade
1213-21

King Louis IX of France's
1st Crusade
1250-4

King Louis's
2nd Crusade
1270

Mamluks capture
Antioch
1268

1175   1200   1225   1250   1275

Mamluks
capture
Acre
1291

Hospitallers
occupy Rhodes
1309

Arrest of Templars
1307-14

Ottoman Turks
enter Europe
1345

Ottoman Turks occupy
most of Bulgaria
1371

1300   1325   1350   1375   1400

Ottoman Turks capture
Constantinople
1453

Christians complete
reconquest of Spain
1492

Columbus sails to
New World
1492

Ottoman Turks
capture Rhodes
from Hospitallers
1528

1425   1450   1475   1500   1525

Glossary

Abbasids   A family of caliphs that ruled in the Middle East from 750 to 1258. Their capital was Baghdad.

Amir   A local Muslim ruler. In Arabic, amir means 'one who commands'.

Astrolabe   A scientific instrument for measuring the position of the stars and the sun. It was used for telling the time and for navigation.

Byzantine Empire   The empire of the Greeks of Constantinople. It was named after Byzantium, the old name for Constantinople.

Caliph   The title of the supreme ruler of Islam. It means both the 'successor' and 'deputy' of Muhammad.

Cathars   A Medieval Christian sect in the south of France. The cathars believed in two Gods, one good and one evil. The Catholic Church saw them as heretics and launched crusades to destroy the whole sect.

Christendom   A term often used in the Middle Ages, to describe all the lands where Christians lived.

Fatimids   A Shiite dynasty of caliphs that ruled Egypt from the tenth to the twelfth centuries. The Fatimids were enemies of the Sunni Abbasid caliphs.

Feudalism   A system of sharing out land that was common in Europe in the Middle Ages. In theory, the king owned most land, but he granted territory to his barons in return for military service. The barons then granted smaller pieces of land to their followers.

Franks   The French. Muslims called all western Europeans Franks.

Heretic   A Christian who holds beliefs that are different from those of the Church.

Hospitallers   Knights of the Hospital of St John, a military order originally formed to look after poor pilgrims. The Hospitallers wore black robes decorated with a white cross that had eight points.

Indulgence   A type of pardon, or forgiveness, for someone's sins. The Pope issued various types of indulgence. Most common was the plenary (or full) indulgence, which freed the crusader from all the punishment awaiting him in the next world.

Infidel   An unbeliever. The crusaders called Muslims infidels.

Jihad   The Arabic name for the Muslim Holy War.

Knight   A lesser member of the nobility in the Middle Ages. In battle, knights were cavalry officers, riding on horseback.

Mangonel   A siege catapult. Mangonels had a throwing arm, like a see-saw. At one end was a cup for holding rocks. The other end had a number of ropes which were pulled down sharply to fire the rocks.

Martyr   Someone who dies for his or her beliefs. Muslims and Christians both believed that if they were killed in the crusades they would be religious martyrs.

Ottomans   A Turkish tribe, named after its founder, Osman. Between the fourteenth and seventeenth centuries, the Ottomans conquered the Middle East and the Balkans.

Outremer   French for 'overseas'. It was

the name for the states created by the crusaders in the Middle East.

Penance   An action performed by Christians to show that they are sorry for their sins.

Pilgrimage   A journey made to a holy place, such as the tomb of a saint. Some people went on pilgrimages as a penance. Others went to ask a favour of a saint, or as a sign of devotion or gratitude.

Saracens   The Greek name for the Arabs. Crusaders called all Muslims Saracens or Turks.

Seljuks   A Turkish tribe, named after its founder, Seljuk. In the eleventh century, the Seljuks conquered Persia, Iraq, Turkey, Syria and Palestine. By the time of the First Crusade, their power was in decline.

Shiites   Muslims who belong to the *shia* or 'party' of Ali. They believe that the caliph should be a descendant of Muhammad through his son-in-law, Ali.

Sultan   Arabic title meaning 'power' or 'ruler'. It was used, particularly by the Turks, to mean a political and military leader.

Sunnis   Members of the main group in Islam, opposed to the Shiites. Sunni Muslims follow the *sunna*, the accepted practice of the Islamic community.

Templars   Knights of the Temple of Solomon, the most famous of the military orders. The Templars wore white robes decorated with a red cross.

Turks   A race from Central Asia which settled in the land now called Turkey. After the eleventh century, some of the most powerful Muslim leaders and soldiers were Turks.

Books to Read

Two of the other books in this series give useful information about the background to the crusades:

Peter Chrisp, *The Rise of Islam*, (Wayland, 1991) This book looks in more detail at the Muslim society of the Middle East.

Mark Ormrod, *Life in the Middle Ages*, (Wayland, 1991) This book examines European mediaeval society of the crusaders.

Jay Williams, *Knights of the Crusades*,

(Cassell, 1962)
This book is quite old, but you may still find it in libraries.

The two books below are for adults, but are fascinating and have good illustrations. The first is eye-witness accounts. The second contains maps of the crusaders' routes and the states they created:

Elizabeth Hallam (ed.), *Chronicles of the Crusades* (Weidenfeld and Nicolson, 1989)
Jonathan Riley-Smith (ed.), *The Atlas of the Crusades*, (Guild Publishing, 1991)

Index

Picture acknowledgements

The author and publisher would like to thank the following: The Bridgeman Art Library, cover and contents page, 13, 15, 18, 27, 32, 33, 38, 40; C. M. Dixon 9, 21, 34, 36 (both), 37; Sonia Halliday 11, 20; Michael Holford 7, 25, 28; The Mansell Collection 16 (both), 17 (top), 29, 31; Ronald Sheridan 4, 12, 23 (both), 24, 35, 39, 41, 43; Werner Forman, 10, 44. All other pictures are from the Wayland Picture Library. Artwork is by Peter Bull.